The A

Whoopie Pies

Whoopie Pies Recipes that will melt your Heart

BY: SOPHIA FREEMAN

© 2019 Sophia Freeman All Rights Reserved

COPYRIGHTED

Liability

This publication is meant as an informational tool. The individual purchaser accepts all liability if damages occur because of following the directions or guidelines set out in this publication. The Author bears no responsibility for reparations caused by the misuse or misinterpretation of the content.

Copyright

The content of this publication is solely for entertainment purposes and is meant to be purchased by one individual. Permission is not given to any individual who copies, sells or distributes parts or the whole of this publication unless it is explicitly given by the Author in writing.

My gift to you!

Thank you, cherished reader, for purchasing my book and taking the time to read it. As a special reward for your decision, I would like to offer a gift of free and discounted books directly to your inbox. All you need to do is fill in the box below with your email address and name to start getting amazing offers in the comfort of your own home. You will never miss an offer because a reminder will be sent to you. Never miss a deal and get great deals without having to leave the house! Subscribe now and start saving!

Table of Contents

Chapter I: Fall and Winter Whoopie Pie Recipes 7

1) Pumpkin Whoopie Pies with Cream Cheese Filling 8

2) Oatmeal Whoopie Pies 11

3) Pumpkin Whoopie Pie with Pecan Filling 13

4) Carrot Cake with Cream Cheese Filling 17

5) Apple Cinnamon Whoopie Pies 20

6) Chocolate Peppermint Whoopie Pies 23

7) Salted Caramel Whoopie Pies 26

Chapter II: Spring and Summer Whoopie Pie Recipes 30

8) Funfetti Whoopie Pies 31

9) Red Velvet Whoopie Pie with Cream Cheese Icing 33

10) S'more Whoopie Pies 36

11) Key Lime Whoopie Pies 38

12) Strawberry Shortcake Whoopie Pies 40

13) Lemon Whoopie Pies 43

Chapter III: Mix and Match Whoopie Recipes 46

14) Banana Whoopies 47

15) Lavender Whoopie Pies 49

16) Traditional Chocolate Whoopie 51

17) Coconut Whoopies 53

18) Vanilla Whoopies 55

Chapter IV: Filling and Icing Recipes for Whoopie Pies 57

19) Marshmallow Cream Filling 58

20) Vanilla Bean Icing 60

21) Vanilla Buttercream Filling 62

22) Cream Cheese Filling 64

23) Maple Filling 66

24) Peanut Butter Filling 68

25) Chocolate Ganache Filling.. 70

About the Author.. 72

Author's Afterthoughts.. 74

Chapter I: Fall and Winter Whoopie Pie Recipes

zzzzzzzzzzzzzzzzzzzzzzzzzzzzzzzzzzzzzzzzzzzzzzzzzzzz

1) Pumpkin Whoopie Pies with Cream Cheese Filling

Pumpkin and cream cheese goes together like peanut butter and jelly!

Makes: 18

Preparation Time: 55 to 65 minutes

Cake Ingredients:

- 3 cups flour, all-purpose
- 1 tsp. baking powder
- 1 tsp. salt
- 1 tsp. baking soda
- 1 Tbsp. ginger
- 2 Tbsp. cinnamon
- 1 Tbsp. cloves
- 2 cups brown sugar, packed
- 3 cups pumpkin puree
- 1 cup vegetable oil
- 2 large eggs
- 1 tsp. vanilla

Filling Ingredients:

- 1/3 cup unsalted butter, softened
- ½ cup cream cheese, softened
- 4 ¾ cup powdered sugar
- ½ tsp. vanilla

zzzzzzzzzzzzzzzzzzzzzzzzzzzzzzzzzzzzzzzzzzzzzzzzz

Instructions:

1: Preheat oven to 350-degrees. Cover the bottom of two baking sheets with parchment paper.

2: Sift together the flour, baking soda, baking powder, salt, cloves, ginger and cinnamon.

3: Cream the sugar and oil together in a separate bowl. Stir in the pumpkin puree until smooth. Add the vanilla and eggs, and stir. Gradually stir in the flour mixture until fully incorporated.

4: Scoop Tbsp.-size dollops of the batter onto the prepared baking sheet. Make sure to keep them about an inch apart. Place the baking sheet in the oven and bake for about 15 minutes.

5: Make the filling by creaming the butter, cream cheese and vanilla together until fluffy and light. Slowly stir in the powdered sugar until everything is well combined.

6: Spread the filling between two whoopies to create the whoopie pies.

2) Oatmeal Whoopie Pies

This delicious oatmeal whoopie pies is a perfect treat no matter what time of year.

Makes: 18

Preparation Time: 60 to 65 minutes

Ingredients:

- ½ cup unsalted butter, softened
- 2 cups brown sugar, packed
- ¼ cup shortening
- 2 large eggs
- 1 tsp. cinnamon
- ½ tsp. salt
- 1 tsp. baking powder
- 1 tsp. baking soda
- 3 Tbsp. water, boiling
- 2 cups quick-cooking oats
- 2 ½ cups flour, all-purpose
- 1 jar marshmallow crème

zzzzzzzzzzzzzzzzzzzzzzzzzzzzzzzzzzzzzzzzzzzzzzzzz

Instructions:

1: Preheat oven to 350-degrees. Cover a cookie sheet with parchment paper and set to the side for the moment.

2: In a mixing bowl, cream the butter, sugar and shortening together until smooth. Stir in the eggs, followed by the baking powder, salt and cinnamon.

3: In a small bowl, whisk together the baking soda with the water until completely dissolved and well incorporated. Stir this mixture into the butter mixture from 2.

4: Fold in the flour, followed by the oatmeal.

5: Scoop Tbsp.-size dollops of the batter onto the prepared baking sheet. Make sure to keep them about an inch apart. Place the baking sheet in the oven and bake for about 10 minutes.

6: Spread the marshmallow over the flat side of one of the whoopies. Press another whoopie against the filling, flat side down, so you have the whoopie pie sandwich. Continue in this manner until all whoopie pies have been assembled.

3) Pumpkin Whoopie Pie with Pecan Filling

This pumpkin whoopie pie recipe with pecan filling blends the traditional fall flavors to create a delicious treat!

Makes: 18

Preparation Time: 65 to 70 minutes

Cake Ingredients:

- 1 stick unsalted butter, softened
- 1 cup castor sugar
- 1 large egg, lightly beaten
- ½ tsp. nutmeg
- ½ tsp. cinnamon
- ½ tsp. ginger
- 1 cup pumpkin puree
- ½ tsp. salt
- 1 ½ tsp. baking soda
- 6 fluid ounces buttermilk

Filling Ingredients:

- 6 large egg yolks
- 30 fluid ounces double cream
- ¾ cup brown sugar, packed
- 1 ounce salted butter, softened
- 3 ounces pecans, chopped

zzzzzzzzzzzzzzzzzzzzzzzzzzzzzzzzzzzzzzzzzzzzzzzzz

Instructions:

1: Preheat an oven to 350-degrees. Prepare a baking sheet by greasing the bottom. Set to the side for the moment.

2: Create the cake portion by creaming together the butter and sugar in a large bowl. Add in the egg and stir until smooth.

3: In a separate bowl, shift together the flour, ginger, cinnamon, nutmeg, salt and baking soda.

4: Gradually stir the flour mixture into the butter mixture. Continue to stir until well mixed.

5: Stir in half the buttermilk and half the pumpkin puree until smooth. Repeat with the remaining buttermilk and pumpkin puree. Fold in the pecans.

6: Place a dollop measuring about 2-inches in diameter of the batter onto the prepared baking sheet from 1. Continue in this manner until you have filled the baking sheet with dollops or have run out of batter. Use the back of a spoon to smooth the top of each dollop.

7: Place the baking sheet in the preheated oven and bake for 10 to 12 minutes.

8: Make the filling by pouring the cream into a pan. Place the pan on the stove over medium heat. Let the cream start to boil while stirring occasionally.

9: Stir in the sugar until completely dissolved. Turn the heat off and let the mixture cool slightly.

10: Melt the butter in a small pan. Add the pecans and toast lightly for about 2 minutes. Turn the heat off and let cool.

11: Whisk the egg yolks together in a bowl. Pour in the cream mixture from 9 and whisk until well mixed. Stir in the toasted pecans from 11. Place the frosting in the fridge for at least 5 hours.

12: Spread the frosting on the bottom of one whoopie pie. Place a second whoopie pie on top to make a sandwich. Continue in this manner until you have used all whoopie pies.

4) Carrot Cake with Cream Cheese Filling

It's really the spices in carrot cake that gives it that delicious fall flavor. And these whoopie pies are perfect for the colder months.

Makes: 18

Preparation Time: 40 to 50 minutes + 30 minutes to chill the dough

Cookie Ingredients:

- 2 cups flour, all-purpose
- 1 ½ tsp. baking soda
- 1 ½ tsp. baking powder
- 1 ½ tsp. ginger
- 1 ½ tsp. cinnamon
- 1 tsp. nutmeg
- ½ tsp. salt
- 2 Tbsp. vegetable shortening
- 6 Tbsp. butter, softened
- ½ cup granulated sugar

- ½ cup brown sugar, packed
- 2 large eggs
- 1 tsp. vanilla
- ½ cup raisins
- 1 cup grated carrots

Filling Ingredients:

- 6 Tbsp. butter, softened
- 8 ounces cream cheese, softened
- 1 tsp. vanilla
- 2 cups powdered sugar
- Pinch of table salt

zzzzzzzzzzzzzzzzzzzzzzzzzzzzzzzzzzzzzzzzzzzzzzzzz

Instructions:

1: Preheat the oven to 350-degrees. Cover the bottom of a baking sheet with parchment paper.

2: Beat the both sugars, shortening and butter together until smooth. Add the egg and vanilla and mix until well combined.

3: Shift together the flour, baking powder, powder soda, ginger, cinnamon, nutmeg and salt together. Gradually stir this mixture into the butter mixture until smooth.

4: Fold in the raisins and carrots. Place the batter in the fridge to chill for at least 30 minutes.

5: Scoop Tbsp.-size dollops of the batter onto the prepared baking sheet. Make sure to keep them about an inch apart. Place the baking sheet in the oven and bake for about 15 minutes.

6: Beat all the ingredients together until light and fluffy. Spread the filling over the flat side of one of the whoopies. Press another whoopie against the filling, flat side down, so you have the whoopie pie sandwich. Continue in this manner until all whoopie pies have been assembled.

5) Apple Cinnamon Whoopie Pies

The combination of apples and cinnamon are common in the fall months so it's only natural to include this recipe.

Makes: 18

Preparation Time: 70 to 75 minutes

Cake Ingredients:

- 1 stick unsalted butter, softened
- 1 cup castor sugar
- 1 large egg, lightly beaten
- 3 cups all-purpose flour
- 1 ¼ tsp. baking soda
- 1 tsp. cinnamon
- ½ tsp. salt
- 1 cup buttermilk

Filling Ingredients:

- 1 cup mascarpone cheese
- 1 1/1 cup cubed apples, peeled and cored
- 1 Tbsp. lemon juice

zzzzzzzzzzzzzzzzzzzzzzzzzzzzzzzzzzzzzzzzzzzzzzzzzzzz

Instructions:

1: Preheat the oven to 350-degrees. Prepare a baking sheet by greasing the bottom.

2: Cream the softened butter with the sugar. Add the egg and stir until smooth.

3: In a separate bowl, sift together the flour, salt, baking soda and cinnamon. Stir in the buttermilk. Gradually combine this mixture with the butter mixture.

4: Place a dollop measuring about 2-inches in diameter of the batter onto the prepared baking sheet from 1. Continue in this manner until you have filled the baking sheet with dollops or have run out of batter. Use the back of a spoon to smooth the top of each dollop.

5: Place the baking sheet in the preheated oven and bake for 10 to 12 minutes.

6: Make the filling by placing the apple chunks into a pan. Add 1 Tbsp. of water and cook for about 15 minutes. You want the apples to be soft.

7: Drain the water from the apples before transferring them to a blender. Blend the apples until smooth. Add the cheese and lemon juice before blending once again until smooth.

8: Spread the frosting on the bottom of one whoopie pie. Place a second whoopie pie on top to make a sandwich. Continue in this manner until you have used all whoopie pies.

6) Chocolate Peppermint Whoopie Pies

Peppermint is a traditional winter flavor that pars well with chocolate to create a wonderful whoopie pie!

Makes: 18

Preparation Time: 45 to 55 minutes

Cake Ingredients:

- 3 ½ cups flour, all-purpose
- 1 ½ cup cocoa powder, unsweetened
- 1 tsp. salt
- 1 tsp. baking powder
- 1 Tbsp. baking soda
- 1 cup unsalted butter, softened
- 2 cups granulated sugar
- 2 cups buttermilk
- ½ tsp. peppermint extract
- 2 tsp. vanilla extract
- ½ cup mini chocolate chips

Filling Ingredients:

- 6 Tbsp. salted butter, softened
- 1 ½ cup powdered sugar
- ½ tsp. peppermint extract
- 1 ½ cup marshmallow fluff
- Red food coloring

zzzzzzzzzzzzzzzzzzzzzzzzzzzzzzzzzzzzzzzzzzzzzzzzzz

Instructions:

1: Preheat the oven to 400-degrees. Cover the bottom of a cookie sheet with parchment paper. Set to the side for the moment.

2: Sift the flour, salt, cocoa powder, baking powder and baking soda together in a mixing bowl.

3: In a separate bowl, cream together the sugar and butter until the mixture is fluffy. Mix in the eggs, one at a time. Stir in the buttermilk, peppermint and vanilla until mixed well.

5: Slowly stir the dry ingredients into the wet ingredients. Keep stirring until the mixture is smooth.

6: Fold in the chocolate chips.

7: Scoop Tbsp.-size dollops of the batter onto the prepared baking sheet. Make sure to keep them about an inch apart. Place the baking sheet in the oven and bake for about 13 minutes.

8: Create the filling by beating the butter until fluffy and light. Stir in the peppermint, salt and two to three drops of the food coloring until well mixed.

9: Add a little of the powdered sugar at a time and beat until smooth. Mix in the marshmallow fluff until the mixture is creamy.

10: Spread the filling between two whoopie cookies to create the whoopie pies.

7) Salted Caramel Whoopie Pies

Salted caramel has become a fall favorite over the past few years and with good reason. This delicious and rick flavor is a great way to bring in the autumn season.

Makes: 18

Preparation Time: 45 to 50 minutes

Whoopie Ingredients:

- 2 cups flour, all-purpose
- ½ cup cocoa powder, unsweetened
- 1 tsp. salt
- 1 ¼ tsp. baking soda
- 1 tsp. vanilla
- 1 cup buttermilk
- 1 cup brown sugar, packed
- ½ cup unsalted butter, softened
- 1 large egg

Filling Ingredients:

- 2 Tbsp. water
- ½ cup granulated sugar
- ¼ cup heavy cream
- 1 Tbsp. corn syrup
- ½ tsp. sea salt
- 6 Tbsp. unsalted butter, softened
- ¼ cup sour cream
- 3 cups powdered sugar

zzzzzzzzzzzzzzzzzzzzzzzzzzzzzzzzzzzzzzzzzzzzzzzzzz

Instructions:

1: Preheat the oven to 350-degrees.

2: Sift together the flour, salt, baking soda and cocoa. Set to the side for the moment.

3: In a small bowl, whisk together the vanilla and buttermilk.

4: Cream together the butter and brown sugar until fluffy and light. Add the egg and beat until well mixed.

5: Gradually mix the buttermilk mixture together with the flour mixture. Fold in the butter mixture and stir until smooth.

6: Scoop Tbsp.-size dollops of the batter onto the prepared baking sheet. Make sure to keep them about an inch apart. Place the baking sheet in the oven and bake for about 10 to 12 minutes.

7: Make the filling by mixing the water, corn syrup and sugar together in saucepan. Place the saucepan on the stove and heat on medium-high. Let the mixture cook while stirring constantly until it develops a golden brown color.

8: While the sugar mixture is cooking, bring the cream and salt to a simmer in a small pan.

9: When the mixture from 7 is done, remove it from heat and let cool for a minute before mixing it into the mixture from 8. Let the mixture cool for 3 minutes.

10: Whisk the sour cream into the mixture and let cool. Once cool, beat in the butter until it is smooth, followed by the powdered sugar.

11: Spread the filling onto one whoopie and top with a second one.

Chapter II: Spring and Summer Whoopie Pie Recipes

zzzzzzzzzzzzzzzzzzzzzzzzzzzzzzzzzzzzzzzzzzzzzzzzzzzzzz

8) Funfetti Whoopie Pies

It's the bright colored sprinkles in the prepackaged cake mix that makes these whoopie pies so much fun!

Makes: 18

Preparation Time: 80 to 90 minutes

Whoopie Ingredients:

- 1 box Funfettit cake mix, prepared according to the back of the box
- 1 ¼ cup flour, all-purpose

Filling Ingredients:

- ½ cup unsalted butter, softened
- ¾ cup marshmallow fluff
- 1 cup powdered sugar
- Pinch of salt
- ½ tsp. vanilla
- 2 ½ Tbsp. rainbow colored sprinkles

zzzzzzzzzzzzzzzzzzzzzzzzzzzzzzzzzzzzzzzzzzzzzzzzzz

Instructions:

1: Preheat oven to 350-degrees. Prepare a baking sheet by lining the bottom with parchment paper. Set to the side for the moment.

2: Make the cake mix as instructed on the box of the box. Add in the flour and mix until well combined.

3: Drop 1 ½ Tbsp.-sized dollops of the dough onto the prepared baking sheet. Place in the oven and bake for about 12 to 14 minutes. Let the whoopies cool before adding the icing.

4: Make the filling by mixing the butter with the marshmallow fluff until smooth.

5: Gradually stir in the powdered sugar until well incorporated. Stir in the salt and vanilla. Fold in the rainbow-colored sprinkles.

6: Spread the frosting between two whoopies.

9) Red Velvet Whoopie Pie with Cream Cheese Icing

Who doesn't like red velvet? This whoopie recipe features the classic red velvet taste with traditional cream cheese icing.

Makes: 18

Preparation Time: 40 to 50 minutes

Whoopie Ingredients:

- 7 ounces caster sugar
- 4 ounces unsalted butter, softened
- 1 tsp. vanilla
- 1 large egg
- 1 tsp. distilled white vinegar
- 1 ounce unsweetened cocoa powder
- 8 ½ ounces flour, all-purpose
- 1 tsp. baking soda
- 8 fluid ounces buttermilk
- Red food coloring

Icing Ingredients:

- 1/3 cup unsalted butter, softened
- ½ cup cream cheese, softened
- 4 ¾ cup powdered sugar
- ½ tsp. vanilla

zzzzzzzzzzzzzzzzzzzzzzzzzzzzzzzzzzzzzzzzzzzzzzzzzz

Instructions:

1: Preheat the oven to 350-degrees. Grease the bottom of a baking sheet and set to the side for the moment.

2: Sift the flour and baking soda together in a small bowl.

3: In a medium mixing bowl, cream the sugar and butter together until fluffy. Add the egg and beat until mixed.

4: Pour the cocoa in a third bowl. Mix in the vinegar, vanilla and red food coloring. Add the food coloring one drop at a time until you achieve the desired shade associated with red velvet.

5: Combine the butter mixture with the cocoa mixture. Gradually add the flour mixture and buttermilk and mix until well combined.

6: Drop 1 ½ Tbsp.-sized dollops of the dough onto the prepared baking sheet. Place in the oven and bake for about 12 minutes. Let the whoopies cool before adding the desired icing.

7: Make the filling by creaming the butter, cream cheese and vanilla together until fluffy and light. Slowly stir in the powdered sugar until everything is well combined.

8: Spread the filling between two whoopies to create the whoopie pies.

10) S'more Whoopie Pies

S'mores are a summer treat favorite, and these whoopie pies capture that flavor and brings it to the comfort of your own kitchen.

Makes: 18

Preparation Time: 80 to 90 minutes

Whoopie Ingredients:

- 1 box milk chocolate cake mix
- ½ cup oil
- ¾ cup water
- 3 large eggs
- 1 box instant pudding mix, chocolate
- 1 container s'mores frosting
- 1 jar marshmallow fluff

zzzzzzzzzzzzzzzzzzzzzzzzzzzzzzzzzzzzzzzzzzzzzzzzzz

Instructions:

1: Preheat oven to 350-degrees. Cover the bottom of a baking sheet with parchment paper. Set to the side for the moment.

2: Mix the cake mix, eggs, oil, pudding mix and water together for about 1 minute.

3: Drop 1 ½ Tbsp.-sized dollops of the dough onto the prepared baking sheet. Place in the oven and bake for about 10 minutes. Let the whoopies cool before adding the icing.

4: Spread the smore's frosting over the flat side of one whoopie cookie. Spread the marshmallow fluff over the flat side of a second whoopie cookie. Press the two sides together. Continue in this manner until you have frosted all whoopie cookies.

11) Key Lime Whoopie Pies

This tropical flavored whoopie pie is easy to make thanks to the use of prepackaged cake mix.

Makes: 18

Preparation Time: 40 to 50 minutes

Whoopie Ingredients:

- 1 package yellow cake mix
- ½ cup vegetable oil
- ½ cup water
- 3 large eggs
- 1 cup graham cracker crumbs

Filling Ingredients:

- 1 14-ounce container whipped topping
- 1 can condensed milk, sweetened
- 6 Tbsp. lime juice
- 1 6-ounce container key lime yogurt
- Green food coloring

zzzzzzzzzzzzzzzzzzzzzzzzzzzzzzzzzzzzzzzzzzzzzzzzz

Instructions:

1: Preheat an oven to 350-degrees. Prepare a baking sheet by lining it with parchment paper. Set to the side for the moment.

2: Combine the cake mix, oil, water, graham cracker crumbs and egg together until well blended.

3: Drop 1 ½ Tbsp.-sized dollops of the dough onto the prepared baking sheet. Place in the oven and bake for about 13 minutes. Let the whoopies cool before adding the icing.

4: Create the filling by beating the condensed milk and lime juice together until the mixture is thick. Fold in the key lime yogurt, followed by the whipped topping. Stir in the food coloring, one drop at a time until you reach the desired color.

5: Spread the frosting on the bottom of one whoopie pie. Place a second whoopie pie on top to make a sandwich. Continue in this manner until you have used all whoopie pies.

12) Strawberry Shortcake Whoopie Pies

Nothing says strawberries better than strawberry shortcakes!

Makes: 12

Preparation Time: 50 to 60 minutes

Whoopie Ingredients:

- 2 ¼ cups flour
- ½ tsp. salt
- 1 ½ tsp. baking powder
- 4 Tbsp. shortening
- 4 Tbsp. butter, softened
- ½ cup brown sugar, packed
- ½ cup granulated sugar
- 2 large eggs
- ½ cup buttermilk
- 2 Tbsp. milk
- 1 tsp. vanilla
- 1 tsp. distilled white vinegar
- 1 tsp. baking soda

Filling Ingredients:

- ½ cup powdered sugar
- 2 cups heavy cream
- 1 tsp. vanilla
- 3 cups strawberries, destemmed and chopped

zzzzzzzzzzzzzzzzzzzzzzzzzzzzzzzzzzzzzzzzzzzzzzzz

Instructions:

1: Preheat oven to 375-degrees. Line the bottom of a baking sheet with parchment paper and set to the side.

2: Whisk the flour, salt and baking powder together.

3: In a large bowl, cream the butter, brown sugar, sugar and shortening together until creamy. Add in the buttermilk, eggs and vanilla.

4: Mix the vinegar, milk and baking soda together in a small bowl.

5: Stir the flour mixture into the butter mixture until smooth. Add the vinegar mixture.

6: Drop 1 ½ Tbsp.-sized dollops of the dough onto the prepared baking sheet. Place in the oven and bake for about 10 minutes. Let the whoopies cool before adding the icing.

5: Create the filling by whipping the cream with a handheld mixer on high. Once stiff peaks form, add the vanilla and powdered sugar and continue to whip.

7: Spread the filling over the flat side of one whoopie. Place some sliced strawberries directly on the filling and top with a second whoopie pie.

13) Lemon Whoopie Pies

These lemon whoopie pies are refreshing, which makes them the perfect summer treat!

Makes: 18

Preparation Time: 45 to 55 minutes

Whoopie Ingredients:

- 2 cups granulated sugar
- ¾ cup unsalted butter, softened
- 2 large eggs
- 2 tsp. lemon zest
- 2 tsp. lemon extract
- 2 Tbsp. lemon juice
- 1 cup buttermilk
- 3 cups all-purpose flour
- ½ tsp. baking soda
- 1 tsp. baking powder
- ½ tsp. salt

Filling Ingredients:

- 8 ounces cream cheese, softened
- 2 ½ cups powdered sugar
- 1 Tbsp. lemon juice

zzzzzzzzzzzzzzzzzzzzzzzzzzzzzzzzzzzzzzzzzzzzzzzzzz

Instructions:

1: Preheat oven to 350-degrees. Prepare a cookie sheet by lining the bottom with parchment paper. Set to the side for the moment.

2: Cream the sugar and butter together. Add the lemon zest. Beat with a hand mixer for about 4 minutes on high.

3: Beat in the eggs, buttermilk, lemon extract and lemon juice. Gradually add the dry ingredients and mix until smooth.

4: Drop 1 ½ Tbsp.-sized dollops of the dough onto the prepared baking sheet. Place in the oven and bake for about 13 minutes. Let the whoopies cool before adding the icing.

5: Create the filling by creaming the sugar, cream cheese and lemon juice together. Spread the frosting between two whoopies.

Chapter III: Mix and Match Whoopie Recipes

The following whoopie cake recipes can be mix and match with the icing and filling recipes found in Chapter 4. This gives you full control over the flavors and allows you to make fun and unique combinations.

zzzzzzzzzzzzzzzzzzzzzzzzzzzzzzzzzzzzzzzzzzzzzzzz

14) Banana Whoopies

This deliciously fruit whoopie can be paired with various icing flavors, including cinnamon cream cheese, vanilla, marshmallow or even chocolate!

Makes: 18

Preparation Time: 50 to 60 minutes

Ingredients:

- 4 ounces unsalted butter, softened
- 7 ounces brown sugar, packed
- 1 large egg
- 1 tsp. vanilla
- 8 ounces ripe banana, peeled and mashed
- 8 ¾ ounces flour, all-purpose
- ½ tsp. baking powder
- 1 tsp. baking soda
- ½ tsp. cinnamon

zzzzzzzzzzzzzzzzzzzzzzzzzzzzzzzzzzzzzzzzzzzzzzzzz

Instructions:

1: Preheat the oven to 350-degrees. Grease the bottom of a baking sheet and set to the side for the moment.

2: Sift the flour, baking soda, baking powder and cinnamon together in a bowl. Set to the side.

3: In a large mixing bowl, cream the butter and sugar together until smooth and fluffy.

4: Stir the flour mixture into the butter cream. Fold in the mashed banana.

5: Drop 1 ½ Tbsp.-sized dollops of the dough onto the prepared baking sheet. Place in the oven and bake for about 12 minutes. Let the whoopies cool before adding the desired icing.

15) Lavender Whoopie Pies

While the flavor of lavender may not be what comes to mind when you think of sweetness, these whoopie pies are delicious and a real treat.

Makes: 18

Preparation Time: 65 to 70 minutes

Ingredients:

- ¼ cup milk
- ½ cup Greek yogurt, plain
- 1 tsp. vanilla
- 4 tsp. lavender flowers, dried
- 2 ¼ cups flour
- ¼ tsp. baking soda
- 1 ½ tsp. baking powder
- ½ tsp. salt
- ¼ cup oil
- ¼ cup unsalted butter, softened
- 2 large eggs
- 1 cup white sugar

Instructions:

1: Preheat oven to 350-degrees. Blend the yogurt, vanilla, lavender and milk together in a blender.

2: Sift together the flour, salt, baking soda and baking powder.

3: In a second bowl, cream the butter, sugar and oil until fluffy. Add the eggs and mix until well incorporated.

4: Gradually mix the flour mixture into the butter mixture until smooth and creamy.

5: Drop 1 ½ Tbsp.-sized dollops of the dough onto the prepared baking sheet. Place in the oven and bake for about 10 minutes. Let the whoopies cool before adding the desired icing.

16) Traditional Chocolate Whoopie

This is the traditional chocolate whoopie that most people have tried. It is my go-to recipe for whoopie pies.

Makes: 18

Preparation Time: 40 to 50 minutes

Ingredients:

- 4 ounces unsalted butter, softened
- 7 ounces brown sugar, packed
- 1 large egg
- 1 tsp. vanilla
- 8 fluid ounces buttermilk
- 2 ounces unsweetened cocoa powder
- ½ tsp. baking powder
- 1 tsp. baking soda
- 6 ¾ ounces flour, all-purpose

zzzzzzzzzzzzzzzzzzzzzzzzzzzzzzzzzzzzzzzzzzzzzzzzz

Instructions:

1: Preheat the oven to 350-degrees. Grease the bottom of a baking sheet. Place to the side for the moment.

2: Sift the flour, baking soda, baking powder and cocoa together.

3: In a second bowl, cream the butter with the sugar until fluffy. Beat in the egg and vanilla until smooth.

4: Gradually fold in the flour mixture, followed by the buttermilk.

5: Drop 1 ½ Tbsp.-sized dollops of the dough onto the prepared baking sheet. Place in the oven and bake for about 12 minutes. Let the whoopies cool before adding the desired icing.

17) Coconut Whoopies

The coconut flavor of this whoopie pie recipe works well with just about any type of icing.

Makes: 18

Preparation Time: 45 to 50 minutes

Ingredients:

- 7 ounces caster sugar
- 4 ounces unsalted butter, softened
- 1 large egg
- 8 ¾ ounces flour, all-purpose
- 1 tsp. baking soda
- 4 Tbsp. shredded coconut
- 8 fluid ounces buttermilk

zzzzzzzzzzzzzzzzzzzzzzzzzzzzzzzzzzzzzzzzzzzzzzzzz

Instructions:

1: Preheat the oven to 350-degrees. Grease the bottom of a baking sheet and set to the side for the moment.

2: Sift the flour and baking soda. Stir in the coconut. Set to the side for the moment.

3: In a large mixing bowl, cream the butter and sugar together until smooth and fluffy. Mix in the egg.

4: Stir the flour mixture into the butter cream. Stir in the buttermilk.

5: Drop 1 ½ Tbsp.-sized dollops of the dough onto the prepared baking sheet. Place in the oven and bake for about 12 minutes. Let the whoopies cool before adding the desired icing.

18) Vanilla Whoopies

Vanilla whoopies are versatile and can be combined with any flavor of filling.

Makes: 18

Preparation Time: 40 to 50

Ingredients:

- 4 ounces unsalted butter, softened
- 7 ounces caster sugar
- 1 large egg
- 1 ½ tsp. vanilla
- 8 fluid ounces buttermilk
- ½ tsp. baking powder
- 1 tsp. baking soda
- 9 ¾ ounces flour, all-purpose

zzzzzzzzzzzzzzzzzzzzzzzzzzzzzzzzzzzzzzzzzzzzzzzzz

Instructions:

1: Preheat the oven to 350-degrees. Grease the bottom of a baking sheet. Place to the side for the moment.

2: Sift the flour, baking soda and baking powder together.

3: In a second bowl, cream the butter with the sugar until fluffy. Beat in the egg and vanilla until smooth.

4: Gradually fold in the flour mixture, followed by the buttermilk.

5: Drop 1 ½ Tbsp.-sized dollops of the dough onto the prepared baking sheet. Place in the oven and bake for about 12 minutes. Let the whoopies cool before adding the desired icing.

Chapter IV: Filling and Icing Recipes for Whoopie Pies

zzzzzzzzzzzzzzzzzzzzzzzzzzzzzzzzzzzzzzzzzzzzzzzzzzz

19) Marshmallow Cream Filling

This filling is the traditional whoopie pie icing and a lot of whoopie pie loves argue that it is by far the best.

Makes: Frosts 18 whoopie pies

Preparation Time: 25 minutes to make

Ingredients:

- 7 ¾ ounces confectioners' sugar
- 4 ¼ ounces unsalted butter, softened
- 1 tsp. vanilla
- 8 ¾ ounces marshmallow fluff

zzzzzzzzzzzzzzzzzzzzzzzzzzzzzzzzzzzzzzzzzzzzzzzzz

Instructions:

1: Use a handheld mixture to beat the butter until fluffy. Slowly add the sugar and continue to beat until smooth. Add the vanilla and mix until well incorporated.

2: Fold the marshmallow fluff into the mixture. Keep mixing until the mixture is creamy and smooth.

3: Use the frosting in your favorite whoopie pie recipe.

20) Vanilla Bean Icing

This vanilla flavored filling works well for a number of whoopie pies, such as the lavender whoopie pie recipe.

Makes: Frosts 18 whoopie pies

Preparation Time: 25 minutes to make

Ingredients:

- 3 cups powdered sugar
- 1 cup unsalted butter, softened
- 1 vanilla bean
- 2 ½ Tbsp. milk
- 2 Tbsp. heavy cream

zzzzzzzzzzzzzzzzzzzzzzzzzzzzzzzzzzzzzzzzzzzzzzzzz

Instructions:

1: Place the butter in a bowl. Scrap the vanilla bean into the butter. Use a handheld mixer to whip the butter and vanilla together for about 6 minutes.

2: Pour in the vanilla extract, milk and heavy cream. Continue to whip until smoothed. Gradually add the powdered sugar, whipping the mixture until light and fluffy.

3: Use the icing as filling in your favorite whoopie pie recipe.

21) Vanilla Buttercream Filling

This traditional vanilla buttercream flavor works well with any whoopie pie recipe.

Makes: Frosts 18 whoopie pies

Preparation Time: 25 minutes

Ingredients:

- 14 ounces confectioners' sugar
- 7 ounces unsalted butter, softened
- 1 Tbsp. milk
- 1 tsp. vanilla

zzzzzzzzzzzzzzzzzzzzzzzzzzzzzzzzzzzzzzzzzzzzzzzzzz

Instructions:

1: Beat the butter with a mixture until smooth and creamy.

2: Pour the sugar into the creamy mixture and stir until mixed. Add the vanilla and stir until well incorporated.

3: Finally, pour in the milk and mix until the icing is smooth.

4: Use the frosting in your favorite whoopie pie recipe.

22) Cream Cheese Filling

Another staple filling for whoopie pies, this cream cheese icing pars well with any whoopie pie flavor.

Makes: Frosts 18 whoopie pies

Preparation Time: 25 minutes to make

Ingredients:

- 8 ounces cream cheese, softened
- 6 Tbsp. unsalted butter, softened
- 1 tsp. vanilla
- 2 cups powdered sugar
- Pinch of salt

zzzzzzzzzzzzzzzzzzzzzzzzzzzzzzzzzzzzzzzzzzzzzzzzz

Instructions:

1: Use a handheld mixer to beat cream cheese and butter together until smooth and fluffy.

2: Gradually beat in the powdered sugar, followed by the vanilla and pinch of salt.

3: Use the frosting in your favorite whoopie pie recipe.

23) Maple Filling

Maple filling pars well with a number of different whoopie flavors.

Makes: Frosts 18 whoopie pies

Preparation Time: 25 minutes

Ingredients:

- 14 ounces confectioners' sugar
- 2 ¾ ounces unsalted butter, softened
- 4 ¼ fluid ounces real maple syrup
- 2 ¾ fluid ounces double cream

zzzzzzzzzzzzzzzzzzzzzzzzzzzzzzzzzzzzzzzzzzzzzzzzz

Instructions:

1: Using an electric mixture, beat the softened butter until fluffy. Gradually beat in the sugar, followed by the maples syrup.

2: Turn the electric mixture speed to low and slowly mix in the cream. Continue mixing until smooth.

3: Use the frosting in your favorite whoopie pie recipe.

24) Peanut Butter Filling

Use this peanut butter filling when you want to add some delicious nutty flavor to your whoopie pies.

Makes: Frosts 18 whoopie pies

Preparation Time: 25 minutes to make

Ingredients:

- 10 ½ ounces peanut butter, smooth or crunchy
- 5 ¼ ounces unsalted butter, soft
- 5 ¼ ounces confectioners' sugar
- ½ tsp. vanilla
- 1 Tbsp. milk

zzzzzzzzzzzzzzzzzzzzzzzzzzzzzzzzzzzzzzzzzzzzzzzzzzz

Instructions:

1: Use a handheld mixer to beat the peanut butter and butter together until smooth and fluffy.

2: Gradually beat in the confectioners' sugar, followed by the vanilla and milk.

3: Use the frosting in your favorite whoopie pie recipe.

25) Chocolate Ganache Filling

This filling recipe is best when made the night before use so it can thicken.

Makes: Frosts 18 whoopie pies

Preparation Time: 25 minutes to make + overnight to thicken

Ingredients:

- 5 ¼ ounces milk chocolate, chopped
- 10 fluid ounces double cream
- 5 ¼ ounces semisweet chocolate, chopped

zzzzzzzzzzzzzzzzzzzzzzzzzzzzzzzzzzzzzzzzzzzzzzzzzz

Instructions:

1: Place a saucepan on the stove over medium high heat. Pour the cream in and bring to a boil while stirring constantly.

2: Add both the milk chocolate and the semisweet chocolate to a mixing bowl.

3: Pour the heated cream over the chocolate and stir by hand. Continue stirring until the chocolate has melted completely.

4: Let the filling thicken in the fridge overnight before using it on your favorite whoopie pie recipe.

About the Author

A native of Albuquerque, New Mexico, Sophia Freeman found her calling in the culinary arts when she enrolled at the Sante Fe School of Cooking. Freeman decided to take a year after graduation and travel around Europe, sampling the cuisine from small bistros and family owned restaurants from Italy to Portugal. Her bubbly personality and inquisitive nature made her popular with the locals in the villages and when she finished her trip and came home, she had made friends for life in the places she had visited. She also came home with a deeper understanding of European cuisine.

Freeman went to work at one of Albuquerque's 5-star restaurants as a sous-chef and soon worked her way up to head chef. The restaurant began to feature Freeman's original dishes as specials on the menu and soon after, she began to write e-books with her recipes. Sophia's dishes mix local flavours with European inspiration making them irresistible to the diners in her restaurant and the online community.

Freeman's experience in Europe didn't just teach her new ways of cooking, but also unique methods of presentation. Using rich sauces, crisp vegetables and meat cooked to perfection, she creates a stunning display as well as a delectable dish. She has won many local awards for her cuisine and she continues to delight her diners with her culinary masterpieces.

★ ★ ★ ★ ★ ★ ★ ★ ★ ★ ★

Author's Afterthoughts

I want to convey my big thanks to all of my readers who have taken the time to read my book. Readers like you make my work so rewarding and I cherish each and every one of you.

Grateful cannot describe how I feel when I know that someone has chosen my work over all of the choices available online. I hope you enjoyed the book as much as I enjoyed writing it.

Feedback from my readers is how I grow and learn as a chef and an author. Please take the time to let me know your thoughts by leaving a review on Amazon so I and your fellow readers can learn from your experience.

My deepest thanks,

Sophia Freeman

https://sophia.subscribemenow.com/

Made in the USA
Coppell, TX
20 August 2021